BLESSED NAMES 7

BLESSED NAMES
WHY WAS HE NAMED AL-BAQIR (A)?
WRITTEN BY:
KISA KIDS PUBLICATIONS

Please recite a Fātiḥah for the marḥūmīn
of the Rangwala family, the sponsors of this book.

All proceeds from the sale of this book
will be used to produce more educational resources.

Dedication

This book is dedicated to the beloved Imām of our time (AJ). May Allāh (swt) hasten his reappearance and help become his true companions.

Acknowledgements

Prophet Muḥammad (s): The pen of a writer is mightier than the blood of a martyr.

True reward lies with Allāh, but we would like to sincerely thank Shaykh Salim Yusufali and Sisters Sabika Mitl Liliana Villalvazo, Zahra Sabur, Kisae Nazar, Sarah Assaf, Nadia Dossani, Fatima Hussain, Naseem Rangwala, Zehra Abbas. We would especially like to thank Nainava Publications for their contributions. May Allāh bless the this world and the next.

Preface

Prophet Muḥammad (s): Nurture and raise your children in the best way. Raise them with the love of the Prop and the Ahl al-Bayt (a).

Literature is an influential form of media that often shapes the thoughts and views of an entire generation. There in order to establish an Islamic foundation for the future generations, there is a dire need for compelling Isla literature. Over the past several years, this need has become increasingly prevalent throughout Islamic centers schools everywhere. Due to the growing dissonance between parents, children, society, and the teachings of Is and the Ahl al-Bayt (a), this need has become even more pressing. Al-Kisa Foundation, along with its subsid Kisa Kids Publications, was conceived in an effort to help bridge this gap with the guidance of ʿulamah and the he educators. We would like to make this a communal effort and platform. Therefore, we sincerely welcome construc feedback and help in any capacity.

The goal of the *Blessed Names* series is to help children form a lasting bond with the 14 Māʾṣūmīn by lear about and connecting with their names. We hope that you and your children enjoy these books and use them a means to achieve this goal, inshā'Allāh. We pray to Allāh to give us the strength and tawfīq to perform our duties responsibilities.

With Duʾās,
Nabi R. Mir (Abidi)

Kisa Kids Publications
4415 Fortran Court
San Jose, CA 95134
(260) KISA-KID [547-2543]

An Introduction to the Blessed Names

Our names are a very special part of us. Many times, they shape our personalities and even explain who we are or the person we would like to become. In this series, you will explore the names and titles of our beloved 14 Ma'soomeen. Did you know that their names and titles were not just ordinary names? They were special because they were given to them by Allah!

Allah has given seven special heavenly names to our Ma'soomeen: Muhammad, Ali, Fatimah, Hasan, Husain, Ja'far, and Musa. Behind each of these names is a heavenly power!

In addition to their names, each of the Ma'soomeen also had special titles by which they became famous. Their titles were often given to them because of the circumstances of their time, but these titles and characteristics were common amongst all the Ma'soomeen. For example, Imam al-Baqir (a) was known for spreading knowledge because he was able to create many new universities and branches of knowledge during his time. However, if the other Ma'soomeen had the same opportunity, they, too, would have spread knowledge and created universities in their teaching circles. In these stories, you will discover some of the reasons why the Ma'soomeen received their specific names or titles.

Many of us share our names with these beloved Ma'soomeen or know people who do. Let's learn about these blessed names and titles so we can strive to be like our blessed Ma'soomeen!

I think al-Baqir means...

_____

An old man struggled as he walked through the sandy streets of Medina. He took turns digging his heavy staff into the dirt and pulling it out as he walked. His old age made the walk slower and more difficult.

He had lost almost all his energy as the burning sun of Medina made the ground radiate with heat. He paused and wiped the sweat off his face. As he walked through the village, he looked down every street and cried out over and over again with a dry mouth, "Baqir! Baqir! Where are you?! I must see you!"

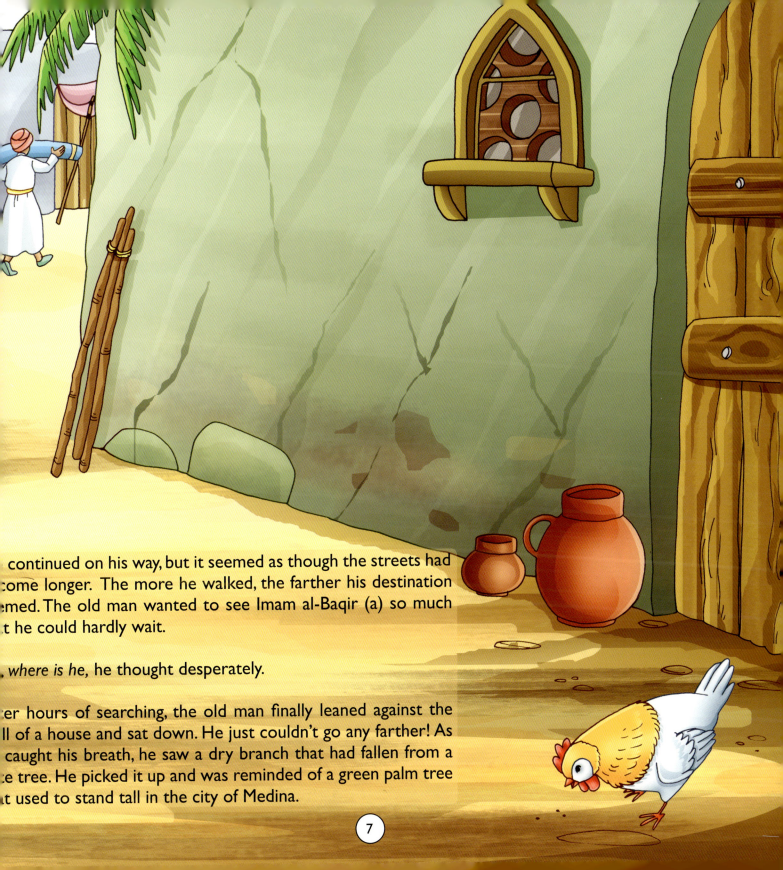

continued on his way, but it seemed as though the streets had come longer. The more he walked, the farther his destination emed. The old man wanted to see Imam al-Baqir (a) so much t he could hardly wait.

where is he, he thought desperately.

er hours of searching, the old man finally leaned against the ll of a house and sat down. He just couldn't go any farther! As caught his breath, he saw a dry branch that had fallen from a e tree. He picked it up and was reminded of a green palm tree t used to stand tall in the city of Medina.

He remembered how 50 years ago, Prophet Muhammad (s) sat near that tree and said to him, "O Jabir, you will live in this world for such a long time that you will get to know my great-great grandson, the fifth Imam (a). His name will also be Muhammad, but he will be known as 'al-Baqir.' When you see him, please give him my salaam because I will no longer be in this world."

Jabir had never forgotten that name, and since that day, he had never stopped looking for Imam Muhammad al-Baqir (a).

However, as he sat on the step on that hot day, exhausted from all his walking, a strange feeling of longing suddenly overcame him. He thought to himself, *the Prophet of Allah (s) always kept his promises. If he has told me that I will see Imam al-Baqir (a), then I will definitely see him, even if there is only one day left in my life. But oh, I just can't wait!*

With that thought, Jabir dug the tip of his staff back into the ground and held onto it as he stood back up. He continued walking slowly again, determined not to give up. Soon, the streets were filled with the sounds of "Baqir! Baqir! Where are you, dearest Baqir?"

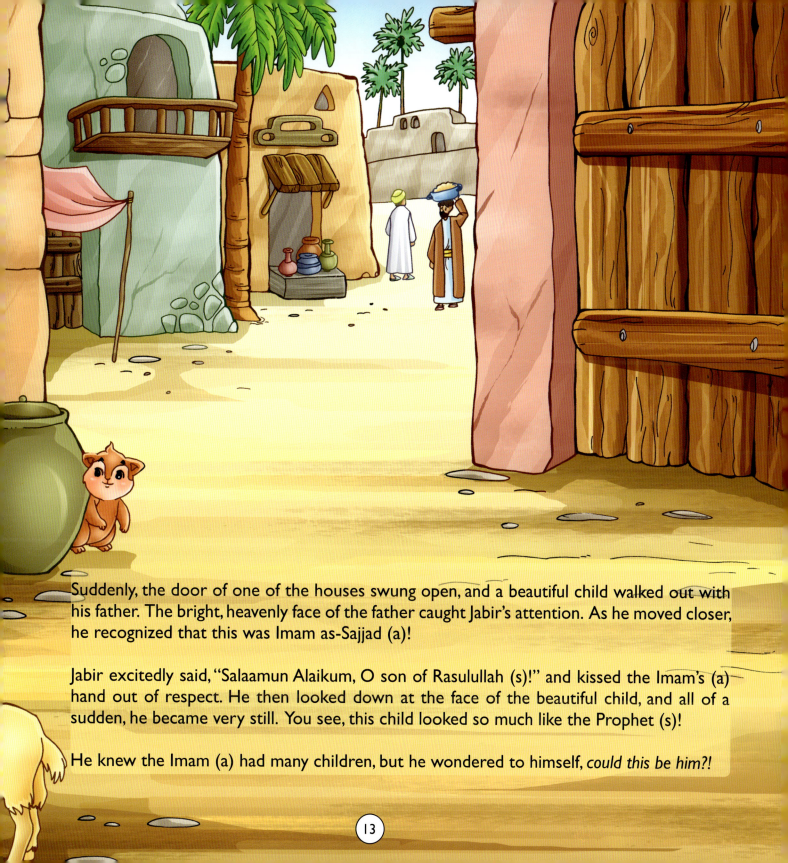

Suddenly, the door of one of the houses swung open, and a beautiful child walked out with his father. The bright, heavenly face of the father caught Jabir's attention. As he moved closer, he recognized that this was Imam as-Sajjad (a)!

Jabir excitedly said, "Salaamun Alaikum, O son of Rasulullah (s)!" and kissed the Imam's (a) hand out of respect. He then looked down at the face of the beautiful child, and all of a sudden, he became very still. You see, this child looked so much like the Prophet (s)!

He knew the Imam (a) had many children, but he wondered to himself, *could this be him?!*

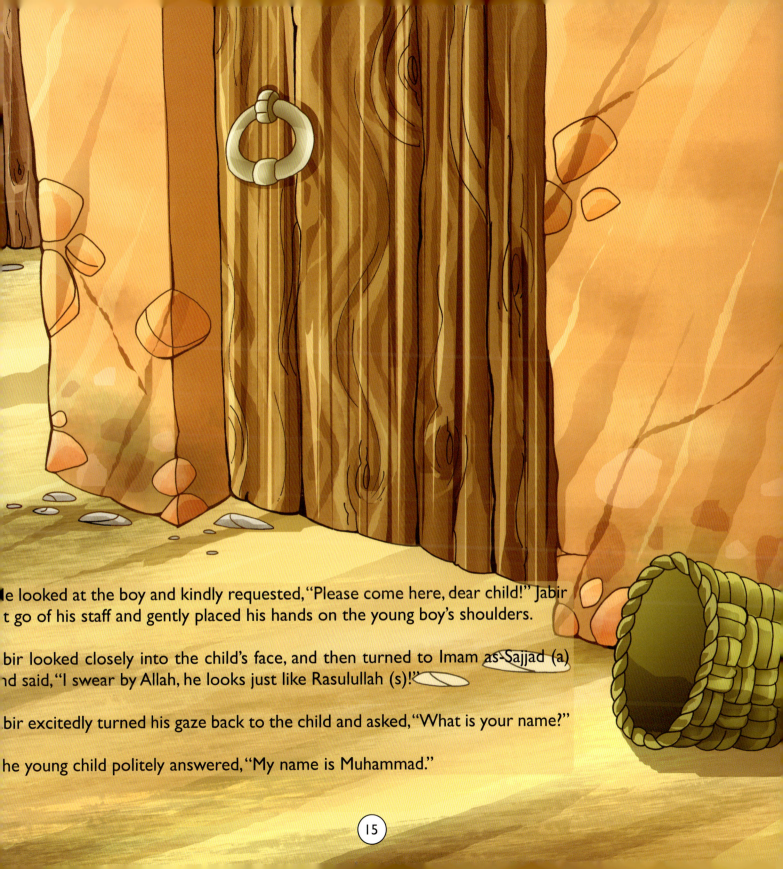

He looked at the boy and kindly requested, "Please come here, dear child!" Jabir
let go of his staff and gently placed his hands on the young boy's shoulders.

Jabir looked closely into the child's face, and then turned to Imam as-Sajjad (a)
and said, "I swear by Allah, he looks just like Rasulullah (s)!"

Jabir excitedly turned his gaze back to the child and asked, "What is your name?"

The young child politely answered, "My name is Muhammad."

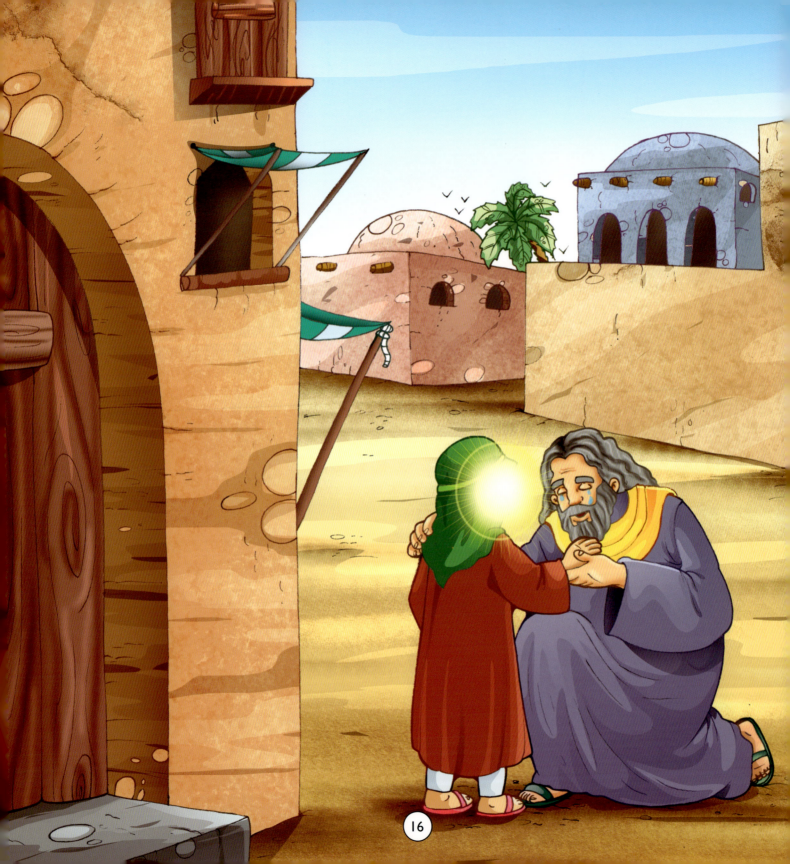

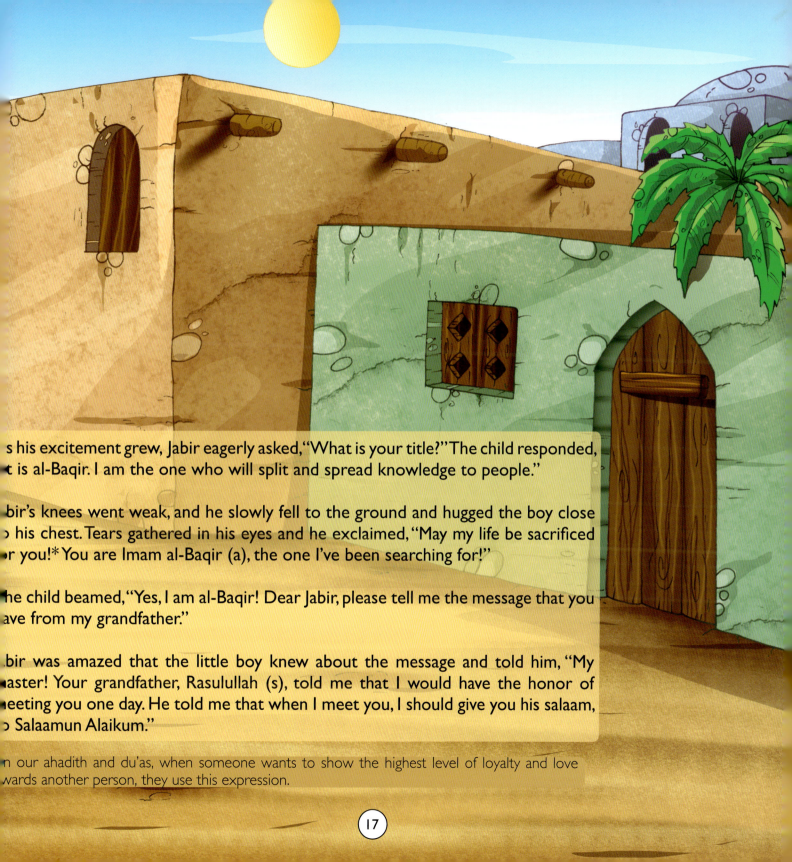

s his excitement grew, Jabir eagerly asked, "What is your title?" The child responded, t is al-Baqir. I am the one who will split and spread knowledge to people."

bir's knees went weak, and he slowly fell to the ground and hugged the boy close his chest. Tears gathered in his eyes and he exclaimed, "May my life be sacrificed r you!* You are Imam al-Baqir (a), the one I've been searching for!"

he child beamed, "Yes, I am al-Baqir! Dear Jabir, please tell me the message that you ave from my grandfather."

bir was amazed that the little boy knew about the message and told him, "My aster! Your grandfather, Rasulullah (s), told me that I would have the honor of eeting you one day. He told me that when I meet you, I should give you his salaam, Salaamun Alaikum."

n our ahadith and du'as, when someone wants to show the highest level of loyalty and love wards another person, they use this expression.

With tears in his eyes, Imam al-Baqir (a) took the tired, old hands of Jabir into his own and gently said, "Peace be upon the Messenger of Allah (s) for as long as the earth and skies remain! Salaam upon you, O Jabir, as you have given me the salaam of the Prophet of Allah (s)."

Jabir spent the entire day watching the young Imam (a) play. As he watched the young Imam (a) feed the animals so lovingly, he knew that this was a very special child. The day gradually came to an end, and Jabir asked for permission to leave.

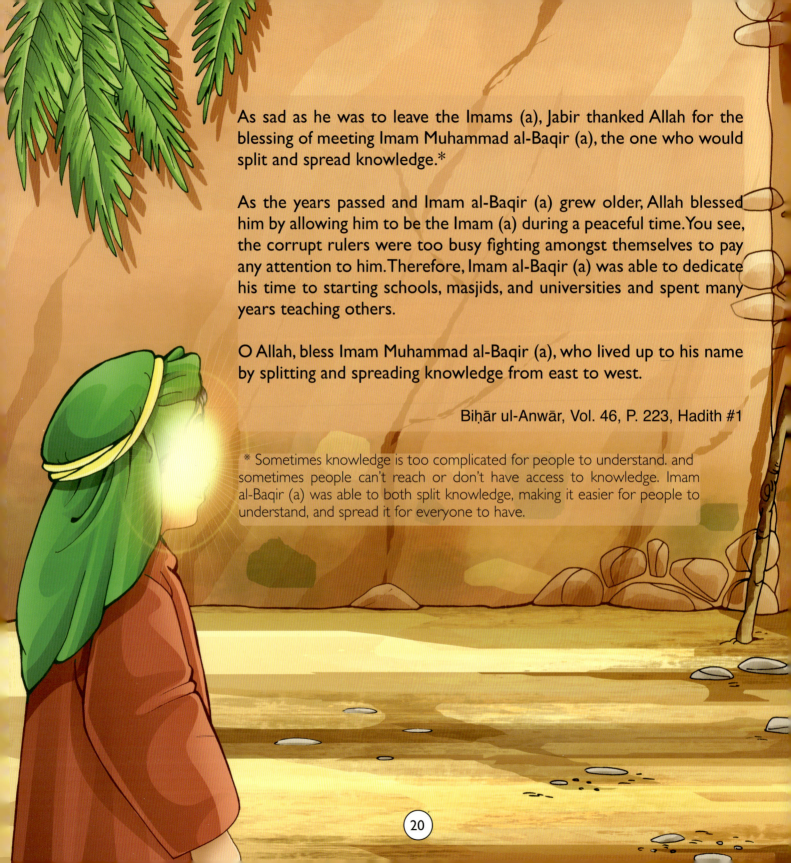

As sad as he was to leave the Imams (a), Jabir thanked Allah for the blessing of meeting Imam Muhammad al-Baqir (a), the one who would split and spread knowledge.*

As the years passed and Imam al-Baqir (a) grew older, Allah blessed him by allowing him to be the Imam (a) during a peaceful time. You see, the corrupt rulers were too busy fighting amongst themselves to pay any attention to him. Therefore, Imam al-Baqir (a) was able to dedicate his time to starting schools, masjids, and universities and spent many years teaching others.

O Allah, bless Imam Muhammad al-Baqir (a), who lived up to his name by splitting and spreading knowledge from east to west.

Biḥār ul-Anwār, Vol. 46, P. 223, Hadith #1

* Sometimes knowledge is too complicated for people to understand. and sometimes people can't reach or don't have access to knowledge. Imam al-Baqir (a) was able to both split knowledge, making it easier for people to understand, and spread it for everyone to have.